Parvus Catechismus Catholicorum

A Small Catechism for Catholics

by St. Peter Canisius, S.J.

Translated from the Latin
by Ryan Grant

©Mediatrix Press
MMXIV

Cover Art: *The Consigning of the Keys*
By Peter Paul Rubens

ISBN: 0692288171

Translated from:
Parvus Catechismus Catholicorum
Published in Ghent, 1756, by John Meyer

©Mediatrix Press, 2014

This work may not be reproduced in any way for commercial purposes or provided for free without permission.

All images are public domain.

Table of Contents

Foreword

by
Fr. Chad Ripperger, SMD, PhD

The whole moral tradition after Aristotle teaches us that when we perform an action in accord with virtue, we experience delight. This applies to the theological virtues as well as the moral virtues and so this is true in relation to faith as it is with any other virtue. Faith is a virtue, we are taught, that resides in the intellect by which we are able to give assent to those things which God has revealed. The Roman Catholic Church is where God deposited those truths of the faith and He left us a Magisterium to teach those truths to every generation, so that even those, even unto this day, who give assent to the teachings of the Church as proceeding not from opinion but faith are delighted to know those truths. The more certitude we have of the faith, the greater the delight.

This is why a catechism, well written, expressing the faith with clarity and precision, is a joy to the person of faith who reads it. This catechism you are now reading is such a catechism. Written by a saint, it contains the basic elements of our faith with clarity. The translation, done by Ryan Grant, captures the clarity of the original Latin, with precision and accuracy. The catechism comes at an important time when many matters of the faith are obscured by many in and outside of the Church. Now

1

more than ever, we live in a time when a good catechism is particularly useful and necessary to the faith. Our hope is that this catechism will provide the reader with an understandable and accessible presentation of the faith and thereby be a joy to him.

Fr. Chad Ripperger
Feast of St. Albert the Great, 2014

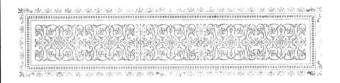

Translator's Preface

St. Peter Canisius is perhaps the sole reason there is a Catholic Church in Germany, even today. Born in Holland, he was a law student and eventually took his Master's degree at the age of 19 in Cologne, Germany when he heard the preaching of St. Peter Faber, one of the first companions of St. Ignatius of Loyola. Immediately, Canisius knew his vocation and entered the Society of Jesus. Although he wasn't among the original companions of St. Ignatius, nevertheless, he was one of the first Jesuits, and the most famous. Apart from laboring for the faith in Germany and Switzerland, he was the first Jesuit to produce any major theological works, and wrote the first Catholic Catechism.

Surprisingly, in the 16th century the Church had not yet produced a Catechism. She had not yet even produced her own edition of the Latin Bible. The Church was slow to pick up on the new technology of printing, and Protestants since the late 1520s, had already produced bibles, tracts and catechisms. Canisius, remarkably and single handedly, challenged and surpassed a generation of Protestant literary output in Germany, holding that just as truly as St. Francis Xavier converted so many in the East, it was a Catholic's duty to labor likewise for the faith in Europe. As we noted above, he produced the first Catholic Catechism. This was the *Summa Doctrinae Christianae*, (Summary of Christian Doctrine), which was a magnum opus in multiple volumes meant for clergy and laymen. He produced a second directed to young men, the *Catechismus Minor* (Smaller Catechism), which is an abridgment of the multi-volume *Summa Doctrinae Christianae.* Later, he produced a third Catechism, the *Parvus Catechismus Catholicorum* (Small Catechism for Catholics) which makes up the present work. St. Peter Canisius produced this work for young children between 9 and 14 years of age. This remains true of this translation, though certainly adults could benefit from its clear presentation and faithfulness to Apostolic Tradition. Therefore, the answers to the questions are more simple than in other Catechisms.

In translating from the Latin, I have taken great care to remain true to the exact formulation of the questions and answers, so as not to lose any of the doctrinal content of the original. For common prayers such as the Our Father and the Hail Mary, I have preserved the standard form Catholics use when praying these prayers. There is an appendix of scripture references which support Catholic doctrine at the end of the work without any commentary, which Canisius arranged for youths to memorize in order to defend the faith when challenged. For these references I have used the Douay-Rheims version, in spite of its shortcomings with respect to modern English readability, because it is the closest version to the vulgate, the basis for Cansisius' work and the common point of reference for both Catholics and Protestants at that time.

This work may prove easier to understand and can work in tandem with other Catechisms, and additionally, was produced by a saint and doctor of the Church. Canisius' reach was so powerful through the centuries in Germany, that Pope Benedict XVI said "Still in my father's generation, people called the catechism simply the

Canisius: He is really the catechist of the centuries; he formed people's faith for centuries."[1]

It is our hope, that reproducing the Catechism of St. Peter Canisius for English audiences will, in like manner, help form and preserve the faith of English speaking Catholics for generations.

Ryan Grant

Post Falls, ID
Fall 2014

---

[1] "On St. Peter Canisius" General Audience Wednesday, February 9th, 2011, Zenit.org, <http://www.zenit.org/en/articles/on-st-peter-canisius>

Madonna enthroned with the Saints
-Peter Paul Rubens

Chapters of Christian Doctrine
Chapter I

On Faith and the Creed.

Who is to be called a Christian, and also a Catholic?

Whoever has been initiated by the Sacrament of Baptism of Jesus Christ, true God and man, and confesses the salutary doctrine in His Church, and not those who adhere to any sects or beliefs foreign to the Catholic Church.

On which things are Christians first to be taught?

On Faith, Hope, Charity, the Sacraments and duties of Christian Justice.

What is Faith?

A gift of God, and light, by which man is firmly enlightened; he assents to all things which God has revealed, and are proposed for our belief by the Church, whether they might be written or unwritten.

What is the chief point of faith, or of all things which must be believed?

The Apostles Creed, in twelve distinct articles.

What are these twelve articles?

These are:

1. Credo in Deum, Patrem omnipotentem, creatorem coeli et terrae.

1. I believe in God, the Father almighty, creator of heaven and earth.

2. Et in JESUM Christum Filium ejus unicum Dominum nostrum.

2. And in JESUS Christ his only son our Lord.

3. Qui conceptus est de Spiritu Sancto, natus ex Maria Virgine.

3. Who was conceived of the Holy Spirit, born of the Virgin Mary.

4. Passus sub Pontio Pilato, crucifixus, mortuus, et sepultus.

4. Suffered under Pontius Pilate, was crucified, died and was buried.

5. Descendit ad inferos, tertia die resurrexit a mortuis.

5. He descended into hell, and rose again from the dead on the third day.

6. Ascendit ad coelos, sedet ad dexteram Dei Patris omnipotentis.

6. He ascended to heaven, and sits at the right hand of God the Father almighty.

7. Inde venturus est judicare vivos et mortuos.

7. Thence he shall come to judge the living and the dead.

8. Credo in Spiritum Sanctum.

8. I believe in the Holy Spirit.

8

9. Sanctam Ecclesiam Catholicam, Sanctorum communionem.	9. The Holy Catholic Church, the communion of saints.
10. Remissionem peccatorum.	10. The remission of sins.
11. Carnis resurrectionem.	11. The resurrection of the body.
12. Et vitam aeternam. Amen.	12. Life everlasting. Amen.

What does the first article of the Creed mean, "I believe in God the Father"?

It shows first in the Godhead a person, namely the heavenly and eternal Father, for whom nothing is impossible or difficult to do, who produced heaven and earth, visible things together with all invisible things from nothing and even conserves and governs everything he has produced, with supreme goodness and wisdom.

What does the second article of the creed mean, "And in Jesus Christ his Son"?

It reveals the second person in the Godhead, Jesus Christ, obviously his only begotten from eternity and consubstantial with the Father, our

Lord and redeemer, as the one who has freed us from perdition.

What is the third article, "Who was conceived by the Holy Spirit"?

The third article proposes the mystery of the Lord's Incarnation: because the same Son of God, descending from heaven, assumed a human nature, but in an absolutely unique way, as he was conceived without a father, from the power of the Holy Spirit, born from the Virgin Mary who remained a virgin afterwards.

Yet, what of the fourth article, "He suffered under Pontius Pilate"?

It treats the mystery of human redemption: for, the same true son of God, after having assumed that human nature, truly suffered for us, and the redemption of us sinners. Wherefore, although the lamb was without stain, nevertheless he was crucified under Pontius the procurator, died on the cross and thereafter was buried.

What, moreover, does the fifth article mean, "He descended into hell?"

It embraces the mystery of the Resurrection of Christ, who, after his life, descended, and was going to free the Fathers from limbo. On the third day after his death, after taking up his body again, he came back to life by his own strength.

What does the sixth article mean, "He ascended to Heaven"?

It conveys the mystery of the glorious ascension of Christ, who, after he had completed the work of our redemption, crossed from this world to the Father, and in triumph ascended into heaven by his own power, and also was placed over all things in the eternal glory of the Father.

What does the seventh article mean, "Thence he shall come to judge?"

It means the last day of judgment, when Christ will descend again from heaven in human flesh, and will make the terrible judgment of the

11

good and of the wicked, and will render to each one according to his works.

What does the eighth article mean, "I believe in the Holy Spirit."

It shows that the third person in the Trinity, the Holy Spirit, who proceeding from the Father and the Son, is one true and eternal God, and reigns with the Father and the Son, hence he is worshiped and glorified together with each.

What is the ninth article, "The Holy Catholic Church"?

It teaches four things on the Church which must be believed. First, that the Church is one, certainly in the one Spirit of Jesus Christ, in one faith and the doctrine both of the faith and the sacraments, in one head and ruler of the universal Church, namely the Vicar of Christ, and the successor of Blessed Peter. Secondly, that she is holy, because she is perpetually governed both by Christ, her head and spouse, to whom through faith and the sacraments she is joined, and by the Holy Spirit. Thirdly, the same is Catholic, or universal, because she is diffused throughout the world, and embraces all the faithful of Christ. Fourthly, and lastly, in this very Church is the communion of Saints. Do not think this only pertains to those who make the pilgrimage on earth, truly, it pertains even to those who have left the mortality of the flesh, or are going to reign in heaven, even those in the flame of purgatory, who are expiating the filth of their sins. Indeed, those who are members of one body help each other by their mutual service, merit, prayers and by the most holy sacrifice of the Mass, and they participate in the power of the Sacraments of the Church.

Next, what does the tenth article teach, "of the Remission of sins"?

It offers the present grace of God to all sinners, lest anyone might ever despair over attaining the forgiveness of their sins, he only need to persevere in the Catholic Church and in turn make use of her Sacraments.

What, moreover, does the eleventh mean, "the resurrection of the body"?

It means that all the dead will be raised back

to life, and confirms the last day of judgment: for before the tribunal of Christ, all will appear renewed in the flesh, that they may receive according to whatsoever each did in his body, whether good or evil.

What, at length, does the last mean, "and Life Everlasting"?

It means the blessed reward to a Christian of faith and virtue, namely immortality, in order that after surviving this life, we might hit upon another, different by far, and truly secure, happy and eternal which has been fixed for believers and those submissive to Christ.

What is the summary of all the articles of the Creed?

To confess the Lord by heart and by mouth, by whom nothing could be more greatly, wisely, or better devised, he who is even one in essence, or divine nature, and in a trinity of persons, namely Father, Son and Holy Spirit, to the extent that these three are one. One, true, eternal, immense, incomprehensible God: from whom, through whom, and in whom are all things. The father is the creator of all things, the Son is the redeemer of all men, the Holy Spirit is the sanctifier of the Church, that is of the faithful of Christ, and the helmsman. Therefore, the three parts of the Creed correspond to this most holy and indivisible Trinity. The first, which is on creation, is applied to the Father; the second, which is on redemption, to the Son; the third, which is on sanctification, to the Holy Spirit.

What is the Church?

The Church is the assembly of all those professing the faith and doctrine of Christ, which is ruled under one supreme head, and one shepherd on earth, subordinate to Christ.

Who are altogether foreign to the Church?

In the first place, Jews and all unbelievers and also apostates from the faith; thereafter heretics, those who, of course, were baptized, but pertinaciously uphold error against the Catholic faith. Besides these, schismatics, those who separate themselves from the peace and Catholic unity itself; and last of all, those who are legitimately excluded from the communion of Saints, from the participation of the Sacraments and the aid of the Church and from divine offices, through Ecclesiastical power, wherefore they are called "the excommunicated".

All those who are separated and foreign to the body of Christ, which is the Church, and hence remain outside of the spiritual life and salvation, unless they should recover their senses, are guilty and merit eternal death, that is Satan. Moreover, while all of these are to be avoided by Catholics, more particularly, heretics and schismatics should be detested and avoided no less than some deadly plague.

At length, what might be a simple, short and upright rule of faith, by which Catholics are distinguished from heretics?

It is this, they confess the faith of Christ and the full authority of the Church; and it behooves them to hold that as certain and fixed, which the Shepherds and Teachers of the Catholic Church have defined must be believed. The others, who do not listen to the Church, should be to you, as Christ himself said "As a heathen and a tax-collector."[1] Indeed he who refuses to have the Church as a mother, will not have God as Father.[2]

---

[1] Matthew XVIII:17.
[2] *"Non enim habebit Deum Patrem, qui Ecclesiam noluerit habere matrem."* St. Cyprian of Carthage, On the Unity of the Church, no .6.

17

The Virtue of Hope
Raphael di Urbino

Chapter 33
On Hope, and the Lord's Prayer.

What is hope?
It is the divinely infused virtue, through which we await with a certain trust in our salvation even the goods of eternal life.

From where do we learn the correct manner of hope and entreaty?
From the Lord's Prayer, which Christ Himself our Lord and Teacher, handed down and prescribed by his own sacred mouth.

Recite through the parts of the Lord's prayer.

Pater noster, qui es in coelis.	Our Father, who art in heaven.
Petitiones	*Petitions*
1. Sanctificetur nomen tuum.	1. Hallowed be thy name.
2. Adveniat regnum tuum.	2. Thy kingdom come.
3. Fiat voluntas tua, sicut in coelo et in terra.	3. Thy will be done, on earth as it is in heaven.
4. Panem nostrum, quotidianum, da nobis hodie.	4. Give us this day our daily bread.
5. Et dimitte nobis, debita nostra, sicut et nos dimittimus, debitoribus nostris.	5. And forgive us our trespasses, as we forgive those who trespass against us.
6. Et ne nos inducas in tentationem.	6. And lead us not into temptation.
7. Sed libera nos a malo.	7. But deliver us from evil.

What does the beginning of this prayer will for

19

itself, "Our Father, who art in heaven"?
It is a little preface, which renders us mindful of the supreme kindness, by which God the Father, through Christ, has admitted us in the number of His adopted sons and heirs. And also we are challenged by this sweet name of Father, both to love him in return, and pray with great trust.

What does the first petition explain in the words "Hallowed be thy name"?
The just and honorable desire of good sons: these always and everywhere ask that understanding, reverence, honor, love and worship of the eternal majesty be advanced in themselves and in others, and at length, whatever pertains to the glory of the supreme and greatest Father.

What do we mean in the Second Petition, "Thy kingdom come"?
We ask for the glory of the heavenly kingdom and eternal felicity to be given to us, that before long we will rule it with Christ in eternity.

What do we mean in the third petition, "Thy will be done"?

We seek the resources of divine grace to be present for us, in order that we might constantly, with alacrity and sincerity, fulfill the will of the Father on earth, as all the Blessed do in heaven.

What do we mean in the fourth petition, "Give us this day our daily bread"?

We ask those things be supplied to us which see to maintaining and sustaining life, whether of the body, or of the soul, as nourishment and clothes, namely the word of God and the sacraments of the Church.

What do we mean in the fifth petition, "And forgive us our trespasses"?

We ask forgiveness and remission of sins, and in turn, being prepared to forgive the sins others have committed against us.

What do we mean in the sixth petition, "And lead us not into temptation"?

We ask in this great weakness of life we may be supported by divine power, and also defended against the World, the Flesh, and the Devil, lest we, succumbing to temptation in whatever way, might consent to sin.

What do we mean in the seventh and last petition, "But deliver us from evil"?

We ask the kindness of God, by which he frees us and defends us from miseries, both of body and soul, either in this life, in so far as it is expedient to our salvation, or in the age to come. And *Amen* is added, this is *fiat* [may it be done], or *fiet* [it will be done], in order that we will show hope and desire for receiving the things which are contained in these seven petitions.

What then, is the summary of the first petitions of this Prayer?

The first four show those things which we should hope in and accept here. Among which, the first and last is the honor and glory of divine

Majesty: next our happiness, to this is added the obedience due to God; last is, the necessary sustenance of body and soul. These things are summarily contained in the first four.

What is the summary of the rest of the petitions?

The second three petitions contain evils which we ought to avert by prayer; namely sins, which shut us out of the kingdom of God, and temptations, which by their strength lure us to sin unless we are protected by divine aid; and lastly the calamities of life, both now and in the future. Therefore, the Lord's prayer teaches at the same time to seek the good and to pray to avert what is evil.

The Annunciation
-Peter Paul Rubens

How do you recite the Angelic Salutation to the Virgin Mary?

Ave Maria, gratia plena, Dominus tecum, benedicta tu in mulieribus, et benedictus fructus ventris tui, Jesus.
Sancta Maria, Mater Dei, ora pro nobis peccatoribus, nunc et in hora mortis nostrae, Amen.

Hail Mary, full of grace, the Lord is with thee. Blessed art thou amongst women, and blessed is the fruit of thy womb, Jesus.
Holy Mary, Mother of God, pray for us sinners, now and at the hour of our death. Amen.

Where does this manner of greeting the Virgin Deipara[1] emanate from?

Firstly, by the example of the Angel Gabriel and of St. Elizabeth, thereafter from the very use and consensus of the Catholic Church.

But what fruit does this Salutation produce?

---

[1] *The word Deipara, -ae* (f) is the Latin translation of the Greek Θεοτόκος (Theotokos), meaning literally she who gives birth to God. It is the classical theological term for Our Lady, which is replaced in Liturgy by *Dei Genetrix*, meaning more literally Mother of God. I have retained it here for theological purposes.
-Translator's note.

It refreshes the memory of the grace of the Most Holy Virgin and of Our Lord's Incarnation, and equally of our salvation, and in addition, advises us, that we might acquire the favor of the gracious Virgin, and also her intercession for us with God.

What do we learn from this Salutation?

We learn of the exceptional qualities and praises of the incomparable Virgin, hence, she stands out for us as inventress of grace and mother of life in so far as she has been loaded with the gifts of God and the fullest virtues, as far as she is at the same time both Virgin and a Mother, in so far as she has been blessed among all women of every time, and in so far as she is the mother of the King of Kings, Christ, our God and Lord.

Moses with the Ten Commandments
-Rembrandt van Rijn

Chapter III
On Charity and the Decalogue.

What is Charity?

The virtue infused by God, by which God is loved for his own sake, and our neighbor for God's sake.

How many are the precepts of Charity?

There are two principle precepts: you will love the Lord your God with all of your heart, with your whole soul, your whole mind and with all of your strength; this is the first and greatest commandment. The second is like unto it: You will love your neighbor as yourself. In these precepts the whole Law and Prophets depend.

By what proof is Charity toward God uncovered?

If you observe the commandments. This is, indeed, the Charity of God, that we should keep his commandments and that his commandments are not heavy. Even Christ himself teaches: Whoever has my commandments and keeps them, he is the one who loves me.[2]

*How is Charity towards one's neighbor
uncovered and recognized?*

Charity is patience, kindness, charity does not boast, it does not act incorrectly, it is not puffed up, it is not ambitious, it does not seek those things which are its own, it is not angry, it thinks no evil, it does not rejoice over iniquity, but rejoices in truth, it suffers all things, believes all things, hopes in all things, and sustains all things.

*Why are the ten precepts of the Decalogue
proposed to us?*

While there might be two precepts of Charity, in which the fullness of the Law is treated, nevertheless the precepts of the Decalogue are added, in order that all should much better understand what pertains to Charity that must be shown both with respect to God and neighbor.

---

[2]John XIV: 21.

What are the precepts of the Decalogue?

1. Ego sum Dominus Deus tuus. Non habebis Deos alienos coram me. Non facies tibi sculptile, ut adores illud.

2. Non assumes nomen Domini Dei tui in vanum. Nec enim insontem habebit Dominus eum, qui assumpserit nomen Domini Dei sui frustra.

3. Memento ut diem Sabbati sanctifices.

4. Honora Patrem tuum, et Matrem tuam, ut sis longaevus super terram, quam Dominus Deus tuus dabit tibi.

5. Non Occides.

6. Non moechaberis.

7. Non furtum facies.

8. Non loqueris contra proximum tuum falsum testimonium.

9. Non concupisces uxorem proximi tui.

10. Non domum, non agrum, non servum, non ancillam, non bovem, non asinum, nec universa, quae illius sunt.

1. I am the Lord your God. You will not have foreign Gods before me. You will not make for yourselves graven images so as to adore them.

2. You will not take the name of the Lord your God in vain. Nor, indeed, will the Lord hold him guiltless who will have done so.

3. Be mindful to make holy the Sabbath day.

4. Honor your Father, and your Mother, that you should be of great age in the land, which the Lord your God will give you.

5. You will not kill.

6. You will not commit adultery.

7. You will not steal.

8. You will not speak false witness against your neighbor.

9. You will not covet your neighbor's wife.

10. Nor shall you covet the house, nor field, servant, handmaid, ox, ass, nor any of the things which are his.

What does the first precept wish, "That you will not have foreign gods"?

It prohibits and condemns idolatry, or the cult of false gods, the art of magic or divination, those observing superstitions, and thereupon every impious cult: it requires, on the other hand, that we should believe in, worship and invoke the one supreme God.

Is one allowed to cultivate and invoke the Saints?

It is permitted, but certainly not in the same manner by which we are commanded to worship and invoke God as the Creator and Redeemer, and giver of all goods; but yet in a far lower degree, certainly as the beloved friends of God, and our intercessors and patrons with Him.

Is the use of the image of Christ and the Saints opposed to this very precept?

By no means, since to this precept, "You will not make graven images," the proviso is soon added: "that you should worship it", obviously from the custom of the Heathen, who set up images of

31

false gods and impiously worshiped their idols. We, however, venerate Christ and the Saints, whom they represent by means of images, from the pious custom handed down by the Fathers.

What does the Second precept forbid, "You shall not take the name of the Lord your God in vain?

It forbids the abuse of the divine name, and irreverence, which is committed by perjuries, blasphemies about God, the Saints, or some creature. Moreover, by swearing without grave cause, truth and reverence.

What does the third precept command, "Be mindful to make holy the Sabbath day"?

It wills the Sabbath or a Feast day in the Church to be celebrated with pious works, which is done by going to Church and by hearing Mass. However, it clearly forbids work during this time and what is due to servile occupations.

What does the fourth precept enjoin, "Honor Father and Mother"?

That we should furnish reverence, obedience, and support to those who are the authors of our life according to God, and at length, that we satisfy them by every kind of duty. Thereupon, it bids, that we should hold officials, not only civil, but even Ecclesiastical, in the place of parents and elders, that we should obey their word gladly, and that we might reverence their power and authority.

For what reason will we revere the power and authority of the Church?

Certainly, if we will have assented to holy and ecumenical Councils, to the received establishments and decrees of the Apostles and the Fathers, to the approved customs of the elders, and thereafter to the supreme shepherds and pontiffs of the Church, so much more, then, do we owe individual observance and obedience. Whereby, to be sure, those who overthrow and defile the divine cult and the Ecclesiastical laws and ceremonies greatly sin, as well as those who belittle Synods and Bishops, and seize the rights and holy places of the priests, profaning sacred things.

What does the fifth precept wish of us, "You will not kill"?

It forbids external force, slaughter and all injury, which could be caused to the body and life of one's neighbor. It thoroughly cuts out and excludes in whatever way, those things pertaining to these: anger, hatred, rancor, indignation, and any of their affects which wound one's neighbor.

What does the sixth precept forbid, "You will not commit adultery"?

It forbids fornication, adultery, and obscenities, illegitimate sexual acts, and whatever is opposed to honesty, and natural shame. For, even anyone who will have lusted after a woman, has already committed adultery in his heart.[1]

---

[1] Matthew V: 28.

What is warned of in the Seventh Precept, "You will not steal."?

Every illicit handling and usurpation of someone else's property, as is done in theft, robbery, usury, unjust profits, wicked deceits, and wicked contracts, at length, in any exchange of business or distributions in which Christian charity is wounded, and a neighbor is defrauded.

What is treated in the eight precept, "You will not speak false witness against your neighbor"?

False witness is forbidden, a lie and every abuse of the tongue against your neighbor, as is done in gossip, detraction, curses, flattery, lies and perjury.

What do the last two precepts forbid, "You will not covet your neighbor's wife nor his goods"?

They forbid the desire for someone else's wife and goods: because it is unlawful not only to seize what is someone else's unjustly and for our own lust, but we ought not even to seek after it in our will, so that we might live content in our own goods, without any envy, rivalry, and lust.

What is the summation, or what is the purpose of the precepts of the Decalogue?"

Without a doubt that God and neighbor should be loved in truth: the distinction of which was made by God was the Symbol of the thing in the two tablets of the Decalogue. In the first tablet three things are taught, which pertain to the love of God; in the second seven are set forth, which pertain to the love of neighbor.

Why do the precepts of the first tablet teach the Charity of God?

Because they abolish and forbid the vices and honor to a cult contrary to God, idolatry, apostasy, heresy, perjury, superstitions, and they prescribe the true and pure worship of God must be faithfully shown in heart, mouth and deed, because when it is done, certainly, the only true God is honored and adored in the cult of true worship.

How do the precepts of the second tablet express charity for one's neighbor?

In this very matter, which concerns our duty toward our neighbor, the precepts are covered in order. Obviously, that we should not only honor our elders, but even benefit all in work, words and will, and we should endeavor to harm no one, and that the body of our neighbor should be regarded, even the woman joined in matrimony to him, his property and his goods.

What is the summation of the precepts on the love of neighbor?

It is this, without a doubt; what you do not wish to be done to you, you should not do to another. But all the things whatsoever you wish that men would do to you, you also do to them. This is indeed the Law and the Prophets.

Are there other precepts apart from the Decalogue?

There are indeed, not only those useful to observe, but even those which are necessary, especially the precepts of the Church, wherein all we Catholic children ought to offer our hearts and minds, to a most holy Mother, as it were, the spouse of Christ.

What are the precepts of the Church?

They are five.
   1. The celebration of all feast days established by the Church.

   2. Reverently hearing the duty of Holy Mass on feast days.

   3. Observing the appointed fasts on the remaining days, and the abstinence from certain types of food.

   4. The Confession of your sins to your own priest, or another with faculties, every year.

   5. The reception of the Most Holy Eucharist at least once in a year, and at that around the feast of Easter.

What fruit does the observation of these precepts produce?

   These precepts, together with the other Ecclesiastical precepts, both being established and commanded, exercise, first of all, faith, humility and Christian obedience: thereupon, they nourish, conserve and adorn divine worship, honest discipline and public peace, and they so wonderfully direct them that, they are successively completed in the Church, beyond which we will merit eternal life, if we will observe these from charity.

The Last Communion of St. Francis
-Peter Paul Rubens

The Adoration of the Lamb
From the Ghent Altarpiece
-Jan van Eyck

Chapter IV
On the Sacraments

What is a Sacrament?

It is a visible sign of invisible grace established for our sanctification. On the one hand there is what we see in a Sacrament, on the other what we receive in it: we see the external sign, but we receive a hidden and Spiritual grace, which is called the *res sacramenti* (the matter of the Sacrament).

How many Sacraments are there?

Seven, which were established by Christ the Lord, handed down by the Apostles, and always having been preserved in the Catholic Church, come down even to us. Moreover, they are these: Baptism, Confirmation, Eucharist, Penance, Extreme Unction, Order and Matrimony.

Why must the Sacraments be venerated and held in the highest esteem?

Truly in the first place, because they were

established by God and Christ our Lord in the New Law: thereupon, because they not only signify the necessary and most abundant grace of God for us, but they even contain a certain sacred instrument of the divine Spirit, and solemnly confer it upon those who receive them. Moreover, because they are a most propitious remedy against sin, or a divine medication of our Samaritan. Lastly, because for the good who have grace, the sacraments preserve, increase and magnify it.

Why are Solemn and Ecclesiastical Ceremonies applied in the Sacraments?

Certainly for many important reasons. First of all, that those observing the administration of the Sacraments might be admonished that nothing profane is carried on here, rather something interior and full of divine mysteries, which they complete with unique reverence. Thereupon, that they might advance the interior worship to the sacraments themselves for those coming to them, which God especially demands, and whose signs, testimony and exercises should be as ceremonies. In addition, that those administering the sacraments might attend their office with greater dignity and fruit, provided that they faithfully hold fast to the institutions of the ancient Church, and the vestiges of the Holy Fathers. It is certain, as a matter of historical fact, that all the ceremonies of this sort were preserved from the times of the Apostles even to us in the Church through a continual succession. At length, honest and religious discipline is retained by them, and public tranquility, which is often of external rites, is fostered by them, quite undisturbed either by change or innovation.

What is Baptism?

It is the first and most necessary Sacrament of the new Law, by which we are enrolled among the heirs of eternal life, because once it is conferred in water, by which we are spiritually reborn, and gain a full remission of sins, we are adopted into the sons of God.

What is Confirmation?

It is a Sacrament conferred upon the Baptized by a Bishop, in which grace is conferred through the Holy Chrism and the most holy words, and a fortification of the Spirit is added, both to firmly believe, and when it might be necessary, to freely confess the name of the Lord.

What is the Eucharist?

It is the Sacrament, in which the true Body and Blood of Christ is contained under the individual species of bread and wine; that we should offer, adore, and consume it.

How many particular doctrinal points of the Eucharist are necessary to know?

There are five; the first is its truth: the second is the conversion of bread and wine into the body of Christ. The third, is the adoration due to it. The fourth, is its offering. The fifth and last, the reception of the same Sacrament.

What is the truth of the Sacrament of the Eucharist?

Without a doubt this, that Christ, true God and man is truly and wholly contained in this Sacrament; when a duly ordained priest has consecrated the bread and wine by means of

45

those secret words, handed down by Christ.

What might be the conversion through those words, by which the Priest consecrates this Sacrament?

It is, that through these very words, with the operation of Christ, bread and wine are turned into the Lord's body and blood, and they are transubstantiated, so that the bread and wine cease to be in the Eucharist.

What is the adoration due to this Sacrament?

It is the same which is rightly owed to Christ the Lord and eternal God, whom we naturally recognize to be present there. And therefore, we humbly venerate this sacrament, as is fitting, not only with the reverence of the body, but even more with the worship of the spirit.

Why is this Sacrament reckoned as an offering?

Because it is a sacrifice of the new Law, and an unbloody offering succeeding the clean offering by means of bloody sacrifices of the Judaic Law, which is offered and celebrated for the living and dead faithful of Christ in the Mass. Wherefore, it becomes that the Eucharist is not only consumed by the faithful, but is even immolated daily by the Priests for sins unto the continual commemoration of the Lord's passion and death, and has always been offered in the Church.

What is preserved in the reception of this Sacrament?

What faith and the authority of holy Mother the Church teaches, namely it is enough for the lay Christian to receive the whole Christ under the species of bread and to attain by this reception, that anyone who does not unworthily receive shall obtain powerful grace and also eternal life, which is the whole and true fruit of this Sacrament; it even becomes more efficacious as often as that sacred and salutary communion is worthily renewed.

What is Penance?

It is the second lifeline after the shipwreck and a necessary Sacrament for those having relapsed, in which the remission of sins and condemnation is sought, and given by the Priests.

How many parts and actions are there for the Sacrament of Penance?

There are three. Firstly, Contrition, or the sorrow of the soul, the detesting of one's sins, and the aspiring toward a better life. Secondly, Confession, or the explication made of one's sins in the presence of the priest, and thereupon Satisfaction, or taking up the restitution and punishment for one's crimes in order to furnish worthy fruits of Penance.

What is Extreme Unction?

It is the Sacrament, in which the sick in great torments of illness are relieved through the sacred oil, and the words of Christ, in order that they might depart from this world more happily. Moreover, even their bodies, if it should be so expedient, may be restored to health.

What is Order?

It is the Sacrament in which the power is

conferred upon Priests and other Ministers of the Church to solemnly and decently attend to their Ecclesiastical offices.

What is the last, Matrimony?

It is the Sacrament, in which a man and woman contracting legitimately, enter an inseparable society of life, and are given divine grace, both that they might honestly and in a Christian manner receive offspring, and educate them, and that they should shun the sin of foul lust and incontinence.

Is there a distinction between the Sacraments?

Naturally: for, Baptism, Confirmation and Order, once conferred may never be repeated, unlike the rest. Baptism is necessarily received by all, but the Eucharist by those with the use of reason, and Penance by those who have fallen back into sin. On the other hand, it is voluntary to make use of the rest, provided that you scorn none of them, or, when it is the time to take them up, that you do not neglect them.

Chapter V
On the duties of Christian Justice

How many duties of Christian Justice are there?

These two, to turn away from evil, or sin, and to do good, or the duty of Justice.

What man can avoid sin, and do good or furnish Justice?

Indeed no man can by himself, rather, by the grace of Christ and the Spirit, an instructed Christian can, and ought to live justly and fulfill the law, in as much as his state of life admits.

How many types of sin are there?

Two: Original and Actual.

What is Original Sin?

It is the sin which we are born with that is absolved through Baptism in Christ.

What is actual sin?

A word, a deed or a desire against or contrary to the law of God or the Church.

How many types of Actual Sin are there?

There are two types: Mortal, so called because it brings immediate death to the soul: (the Soul, which sinned, itself will die); and Venial, so called because it is easily given pardon: and without which not even the just man lives.

By what three steps are we led to sin?

By these three: Suggestion, Delight and Consent, or the deliberate will to sin.

What are the highest degrees of sinners?

They consist in those who, with knowledge and awareness, sin from pure malice. Moreover, those who boast in their sin, and who groan against warnings, and who altogether scorn salutary counsel.

51

Why must we flee from sin?

Because it offends the Lord God, robs us of the supreme good, and brings the worst evil to the sinner, while it abolishes divine fruition which is never to be recovered, and brings punishment and eternal calamities for man.

Which sins are called "Capital sins"?

Those from which all other sins set out, as from a source or font.

How many Capital[2] sins are there?

Seven: Pride, Avarice, Lust, Envy, Gluttony, Anger, and Sloth.

How can these sins be conquered and avoided?

If we cooperate with the grace of Jesus Christ, trusting in the losses and dangers of sins, and exercising the seven virtues opposed to these sins.

---

[2] These sins are today called the "Seven Deadly sins", but The language in use in 16th century has been retained. -Translator's note.

*Which virtues are opposed to the Capital sins?^*

These seven: Humility, Liberality, Chastity, Kindness, Temperance, Patience, and Devotion, that is attentive Piety.

Which sins are said to committed against the Holy Spirit?

Those which in their malice so exclude grace, that they can be remitted neither in this life, except by an exceptional excellence, nor in the next.

How many sins are there against the Holy Ghost?

Six: Presumption of God's mercy, or of the impunity of sin; Despair; Assailing of the recognition of truth, Jealousy of fraternal charity, Obstinacy; and Final Impenitence.

Which sins are said to cry out to Heaven?

Those which in themselves are vehemently abominable, and openly violate the laws of humane Charity, wherein they are regarded to cry out for vengeance, and are often divinely avenged in this life in terrible ways.

How many are the sins crying to heaven for vengeance?

These four: Voluntary Homicide, the Sin of Sodom, Oppression of the poor, of widows and orphan girls, and lastly, Defrauding the wages of a laborer.

Which sins are said to be another's?

Those which indeed are committed by others, but while we were the authors, or helpers in any way, or at least did not impede them, thus they are imputed even to us.

How many ways are another's sins imputed to us?

In these nine ways: Counsel, Command, Consent, Provocation, Praise or Adulation, Silence at another's fault, Connivance or Indulgence, Participation in another's deed, and the Perverse defense of another's deed.

What are works of the flesh?

Those which men who live according to the flesh usually commit, deteriorating from the spiritual sons of God.

What are the works of the flesh?

St. Paul examines them in this way: "The works of the flesh are manifest, which are, Fornication, Foulness, Unchastity, Lust, Servitude to idols, Sorcery, Enmity, Contentions, Rivalries, Quarrels, Dissensions, Sects, Envy, Homicide, Drunkenness, Revelry and the like which I preach to you, I have preached: because, those who do such things will not attain the kingdom of God."[3]

---

[3] Galatians V:19.

Is it enough for a Christian to flee evil and avoid sin?

By no means, rather it is necessary also to do good and exercise the virtues. Besides, for one to know good, and not do it, is a sin.

What good must a Christian do?

Certainly, in general, whatever good that natural law, divine law or human law commands or shows, but in particular each ought to excel in the duty proper to his vocation and combine the grace received from God with the action of graces. Indeed, "every tree, which does not bear good fruit, will be cut down, and thrown into the fire."[4]

What particular kinds of good works are there?

Those in which one lives soberly, justly and piously in this life, and those which in the same manner, the just are more and more justified, and the holy are day by day sanctified.

---

[4] Matthew VII:19.

How many kinds of good works are there?

Three: namely Fasting, Almsgiving or Mercy, and Prayer, about which we read thus: "Prayer is good with Fasting and Almsgiving."[5]

---

[5]Tobit XII:8.

The Seven Works of Mercy
-Michaelangelo Merisi da Caravaggio

What is the fruit of good works?

They hold the promise and reward of this and eternal life, they please God, preserve and increase grace, and thereupon ratify and confirm the vocation of a Christian man.

What is fasting?

It is to abstain from meat on certain days, according to the custom and command of the Church, and to live more frugally on that day, content with the refreshment of merely one meal. But if you should take this noun more generally, *Fasting* is a castigation of the body, taken up with piety, in order that either the flesh should be made subject to the spirit, or obedience might be exercised, or the grace of God should be obtained.

What is prayer?

It is the elevation of the mind to God, through which either we avert evil, or ask goods for others, or we bless God.

What is Almsgiving, or Mercy?

It is the good work, in which we come to the aid of another from the affect of pity.

How many kinds of Almsgiving, or Mercy, are there?

They are two-fold; on the one hand there are the corporal works of Mercy, while on the other the spiritual: because they look to lift up either the corporal or the spiritual misery of a neighbor.

How many corporal works of Mercy are there?

There are seven, Feeding the hungry, giving drink to the thirsty, to clothe the naked, to set captives free, to visit the sick, to receive travelers in hospitality, and to burry the dead.

What are the most excellent of all virtues?

Truly after those Theological virtues, which we have already spoken of, Faith, Hope, and Charity, the most excellent are the Cardinal virtues, which are becoming of a Christian.

Which are called the Cardinal Virtues?

Those which are fonts of the others and the hinges containing every rule of honest life.

How many Cardinal virtues are there?

There are four, Prudence, Justice, Temperance, Fortitude: by which a man attains such a state in Christ, that he might endure his whole life wisely, justly, temperately, and bravely, and he might please God.

Which gifts are said to be of the Holy Spirit?

Those seven which the Prophet witnessed to have rested upon Christ, and just as from a font of all grace are derived from him, onto others: they are the gift of wisdom, of intellect, counsel, knowledge, fortitude, piety and fear of the Lord.

What are those which are called the fruits of the Spirit?

Those which pious living men work according to the spirit, and through which spiritual men are discerned from carnal.

What are the fruits of the Spirit?

They are thus enumerated by the Apostle Paul: "Charity, Joy, Peace, Patience, Forbearance, Goodness, Mildness, Faith, Modesty, Continence, Chastity."[6]

What are the Evangelical beatitudes?

Those by which, on account of what is in the Gospel, even men who appear altogether miserable and unhappy, are pronounced blessed and happy.

How many Evangelical beatitudes are there?

There are eight, which Christ so handed down on the mountain.

1. Blessed are the poor in spirit, because theirs is the kingdom of heaven.
2. Blessed are the meek, because they will possess the earth.
3. Blessed are those who mourn, for they will be consoled.
4. Blessed are those who hunger and thirst

---

[6] Galatians V:22.

for justice, because these will be satisfied.

5. Blessed are the merciful, for they will attain mercy.

6. Blessed are the pure in heart, because they will see God.

7. Blessed are the peacemakers, because they will be called sons of God.

8. Blessed are those who suffer persecution on account of justice, because theirs is the kingdom of heaven.

What are the Evangelical counsels?

Certainly, those which, according to the Gospel, while not necessary for salvation, nevertheless, are more expedient and useful to those receiving them. They are not proposed by Christ as a command, but as counsel.

How many Evangelical counsels are there?

There are three principle ones, namely, Voluntary Poverty, Perpetual Chastity, and Complete Obedience, which is furnished by religious men for God's sake.

What are the last things of man called?

Those which happen to a man at the end; namely Death, Judgment, hell and the glory of Heaven, about which a Wise man thus teaches: "In all your works be mindful of your last things, and you also not sin."[7]

---

[7]"In omnibus operibus tuis, memorare novissima tua." Ecclesiasticus (Sirach) VII:40.

Testimonies of the Holy Scriptures

To be held always in readiness against the Heretics.

The following are quotes from Scripture arranged by St. Peter Canisius himself, in order to assist a Catholic in defending doctrine with Scriptural evidence. -Editor

Deuteronomy XVII: 6-11.

In ore duorum aut trium testium peribit qui interficietur. Nemo occidatur, uno contra se dicente testimonium. Manus testium prima interficiet eum, et manus reliqui populi extrema mittetur: ut auferas malum de medio tui. Si difficile et ambiguum apud te judicium esse perspexeris inter sanguinem et sanguinem, causam et causam, lepram et lepram: et judicum intra portas tuas videris verba variari: surge, et ascende ad locum, quem elegerit Dominus Deus tuus. Veniesque ad sacerdotes Levitici generis, et ad judicem qui fuerit illo tempore: quaeresque ab eis, qui indicabunt tibi judicii veritatem. Et facies quodcumque dixerint qui

By the mouth of two or three witnesses shall he die that is to be slain. Let no man be put to death when only one beareth witness against him. The hands of the witnesses shall be first upon him to kill him, and afterwards the hands of the rest of the people: that thou mayest take away the evil out of the midst of thee. If thou perceive that there be among you a hard and doubtful matter in judgment between blood and blood, cause and cause, leprosy and leprosy: and thou see that the words of the judges within thy gates do vary: arise, and go up to the place, which the Lord thy God shall choose. And thou shalt come to the priests of the Levitical race, and to the

praesunt loco quem elegerit Dominus, et docuerint te juxta legem ejus, sequerisque sententiam eorum, nec declinabis ad dexteram neque ad sinistram.

judge, that shall be at that time: and thou shalt ask of them, and they shall shew thee the truth of the judgment. And thou shalt do whatsoever they shall say, that preside in the place, which the Lord shall choose, and what they shall teach thee, according to his law; and thou shalt follow their sentence: neither shalt thou decline to the right hand nor to the left hand.

Deuteronomy XVII: 12-13.

Qui autem superbierit, nolens obedire sacerdotis imperio, qui eo tempore ministrat Domino Deo tuo, et decreto judicis, morietur homo ille, et auferes malum de Israel: cunctusque populus audiens timebit, ut nullus deinceps intumescat superbia.

But he that will be proud, and refuse to obey the commandment of the priest, who ministereth at that time to the Lord thy God, and the decree of the judge, that man shall die, and thou shalt take away the evil from Israel: And all the people hearing it shall fear, that no one afterwards swell with pride.

Deuteronomy XXXII: 7.

Interroga patrem tuum, et annuntiabit tibi: majores tuos, et dicent tibi.

Ask thy father, and he will declare to thee: thy elders and they will tell thee.

Jeremiah VI: 16.

Haec dicit Dominus: State super vias, et videte, et interrogate de semitis antiquis quae sit via bona, et ambulate in ea: et invenietis refrigerium animabus vestris.

Thus saith the Lord: Stand ye on the ways, and see and ask for the old paths which is the good way, and walk ye in it: and you shall find refreshment for your souls. And they said: we will not walk.

Malachi II: 7.

Labia enim sacerdotis custodient scientiam, et legem requirent ex ore ejus, quia angelus Domini exercituum est.

For the lips of the priest shall keep knowledge, and they shall seek the law at his mouth: because he is the angel of the Lord of hosts.

Proverbs I: 9.

Audi, fili mi, disciplinam patris tui, et ne dimittas legem matris tuae: Ut addatur gratia capiti tuo, et torques collo tuo.

My son, hear the instruction of thy father, and forsake not the law of thy mother: That grace may be added to thy head, and a chain of gold to thy neck.

Proverbs VI: 20-21.

Conserva, fili mi, praecepta patris tui, et ne dimittas legem matris tuae. Liga ea in corde tuo jugiter, et circumda gutturi tuo.

My son, keep the commandments of thy father, and forsake not the law of thy mother. Bind them in thy heart continually, and put them about thy neck.

67

Proverbs XXII: 28.

Ne transgrediaris terminos antiquos, quos posuerunt patres tui.	Pass not beyond the ancient bounds which thy fathers have set.

Ecclesiasticus (Sirach) VIII: 11.

Non te praetereat narratio seniorum, ipsi enim didicerunt a patribus suis: Quoniam ab ipsis disces intellectum, et in tempore necessitatis dare responsum.	Let not the discourse of the ancients escape thee, for they have learned of their fathers: For of them thou shalt learn understanding, and to give an answer in time of need.

Matthew XXIV: 4, 11, 23, 13, 26.

Videte ne quis vos seducat: surgent enim multi pseudo Prophetae, et seducent multos. Tunc si quis vobis dixerit: Ecce hic est Christus, aut illic: nolite credere: et quoniam abundabit iniquitas, refrigescet charitas multorum. Quo autem perseveraverit usque in finem, hic salvus erit. Si ergo dixerint vobis: Ecce in deserto est, nolite exire. Ecce in penetralibus, nolite credere.	Take heed that no man seduce you: many false prophets shall rise, and shall seduce many. Then if any man shall say to you: Lo here is Christ, or there, do not believe him. And because iniquity hath abounded, the charity of many shall grow cold. But he that shall persevere to the end, he shall be saved. If therefore they shall say to you: Behold he is in the desert, go ye not out: Behold he is in the closets, believe it not.

Luke X: 16.

Qui vos audit, me audit: et qui vos spernit, me spernit. Qui autem me spernit, spernit eum qui misit me.

He that heareth you, heareth me; and he that despiseth you, despiseth me; and he that despiseth me, despiseth him that sent me.

Matthew XXIII: 3.

Omnia ergo quaecumque dixerint vobis, servate, et facite: secundum opera vero eorum nolite facere: dicunt enim, et non faciunt.

All things therefore whatsoever they shall say to you, observe and do: but according to their works do ye not; for they say, and do not.

Matthew XVI: 18-19.

Et ego dico tibi, quia tu es Petrus, et super hanc petram aedificabo Ecclesiam meam, et portae inferi non praevalebunt adversus eam. Et tibi dabo claves regni caelorum. Et quodcumque ligaveris super terram, erit ligatum et in caelis: et quodcumque solveris super terram, erit solutum et in caelis.

And I say to thee: That thou art Peter; and upon this rock I will build my church, and the gates of hell shall not prevail against it. And I will give to thee the keys of the kingdom of heaven. And whatsoever thou shalt bind upon earth, it shall be bound also in heaven: and whatsoever thou shalt loose upon earth, it shall be loosed also in heaven.

Luke XXII: 31-32.

Simon, ecce Satanas expetivit vos ut cribraret sicut triticum:

Simon, Simon, behold Satan hath desired to have you, that

69

Ego autem rogavi pro te ut non deficiat fides tua: et tu aliquando conversus, confirma fratres tuos.

he may sift you as wheat: But I have prayed for thee, that thy faith fail not: and thou, being once converted, confirm thy brethren.

John XXI: 15, 17.

Simon Joannis, diligis me? Pasce agnos meos; pasce oves meas.

Simon son of John, lovest thou me? Feed my lambs; feed my sheep.

Matthew XXVIII:20.

Et ecce ego vobiscum sum omnibus diebus, usque ad consummationem saeculi.

And behold I am with you all days, even to the consummation of the world.

John XIV: 16-1.

Et ego rogabo Patrem, et alium Paraclitum dabit vobis, ut maneat vobiscum in aeternum, Spiritum veritatis, quem mundus non potest accipere, quia non videt eum, nec scit eum: vos autem cognoscetis eum.

And I will ask the Father, and he shall give you another Paraclete, that he may abide with you for ever. The spirit of truth, whom the world cannot receive, because it seeth him not, nor knoweth him: but you shall know him.

John XIV: 18; 26.

Non relinquam vos orphanos: veniam ad vos. Paraclitus autem Spiritus Sanctus, quem

I will not leave you orphans, I will come to you. But the Paraclete, the Holy Ghost,

70

mittet Pater in nomine meo, ille vos docebit omnia, et suggeret vobis omnia quaecumque dixero vobis.

whom the Father will send in my name, he will teach you all things, and bring all things to your mind, whatsoever I shall have said to you.

John XVI: 12-13

Adhuc multa habeo vobis dicere, sed non potestis portare modo. Cum autem venerit ille Spiritus veritatis, docebit vos omnem veritatem.

I have yet many things to say to you: but you cannot bear them now. But when he, the Spirit of truth, is come, he will teach you all truth.

John XVII: 20-21.

Non pro eis rogo tantum, sed et pro eis qui credituri sunt per verbum eorum in me: Ut omnes unum sint, sicut tu Pater in me, et ego in te, ut et ipsi in nobis unum sint.

And not for them only do I pray, but for them also who through their word shall believe in me; That they all may be one, as thou, Father, in me, and I in thee; that they also may be one in us; that the world may believe that thou hast sent me.

Matthew XVIII: 17.

Si autem ecclesiam non audierit, sit tibi sicut ethnicus et publicanus.

And if he will not hear the church, let him be to thee as the heathen and publican.

71

2 Peter II: 1-2.

Fuerunt vero et pseudoprophetae in populo, sicut et in vobis erunt magistri mendaces, qui introducent sectas perditionis: et eum qui emit eos, Dominum negant, superducentes sibi celerem perditionem. Et multi sequentur eorum luxurias, per quos via veritatis blasphemabitur: qui in errore conversantur: Libertatem illis promittentes, cum ipsi servi sint corruptioni.

But there were also false prophets among the people, even as there shall be among you lying teachers, who shall bring in sects of perdition, and deny the Lord who bought them: bringing upon themselves swift destruction. And many shall follow their riotousnesses, through whom the way of truth shall be evil spoken of; promising them liberty, whereas they themselves are the slaves of corruption.

2 Peter III: 3.

Hoc primum scientes, quod venient in novissimis diebus in deceptione illusores, juxta proprias concupiscentias ambulantes.

Knowing this first, that in the last days there shall come deceitful scoffers, walking after their own lusts.

2 John I: 6-7; 10.

Hoc est enim mandatum, ut quemadmodum audistis ab initio, in eo ambuletis. Quoniam multi seductores exierunt in mundum... Omnis qui recedit, et non permanet in doctrina Christi, Deum non habet. Si quis venit ad vos, et

For this is the commandment, that, as you have heard from the beginning, you should walk in the same: For many seducers are gone out into the world... Whosoever revolteth, and continueth not in the doctrine of Christ, hath not God. If any

hanc doctrinam non affert, nolite recipere eum in domum, nec Ave ei dixeritis.

man come to you, and bring not this doctrine, receive him not into the house nor say to him, God speed you.

2 Timothy IV: 3.

Erit enim tempus, cum sanam doctrinam non sustinebunt, sed ad sua desideria coacervabunt sibi magistros, prurientes auribus.

For there shall be a time, when they will not endure sound doctrine; but, according to their own desires, they will heap to themselves teachers, having itching ears.

Romans XVI: 17.

Rogo autem vos fratres, ut observetis eos qui dissensiones et offendicula, praeter doctrinam, quam vos didicistis, faciunt, et declinate ab illis. Hujuscemodi enim Christo Domino nostro non serviunt, sed suo ventri: et per dulces sermones et benedictiones seducunt corda innocentium.

Now I beseech you, brethren, to mark them who make dissensions and offences contrary to the doctrine which you have learned, and avoid them. For they that are such, serve not Christ our Lord, but their own belly; and by pleasing speeches and good words, seduce the hearts of the innocent.

2 Thessalonians III: 6.

Denuntiamus autem vobis, fratres, in nomine Domini nostri Jesu Christi, ut subtrahatis vos ab omni fratre

And we charge you, brethren, in the name of our Lord Jesus Christ, that you withdraw yourselves from every brother

73

ambulante inordinate, et non secundum traditionem, quam acceperunt a nobis.

walking disorderly, and not according to the tradition which they have received of us.

2 Thessalonians II: 14.

Itaque fratres, state: et tenete traditiones, quas didicistis, sive per sermonem, sive per epistolam nostram.

Therefore, brethren, stand fast; and hold the traditions which you have learned, whether by word, or by our epistle.

1 Corinthians XI:1 9.

Oportet et haereses esse, ut et qui probati sunt, manifesti fiant in vobis.

There must be also heresies: that they also, who are approved, may be made manifest among you.

Titus III: 6.

Haereticum hominem post unam et secundam correptionem devita: Sciens quia subversus est, qui ejusmodi est, et delinquit, cum sit proprio judicio condemnatus.

A man that is a heretic, after the first and second admonition, avoid: Knowing that he, that is such a one, is subverted, and sinneth, being condemned by his own judgment.

1 Corinthians XI: 16.

Si quis autem videtur contentiosus esse: nos talem consuetudinem non habemus, neque ecclesia Dei.

But if any man seem to be contentious, we have no such custom, nor the church of God.

74

1 Timothy III: 14.

Haec tibi scribo, sperans me ad te venire cito: Si autem tardavero, ut scias quomodo oporteat te in domo Dei conversari, quae est ecclesia Dei vivi, columna et firmamentum veritatis.

These things I write to thee, hoping that I shall come to thee shortly. But if I tarry long, that thou mayest know how thou oughtest to behave thyself in the house of God, which is the church of the living God, the pillar and ground of the truth.

Hebrews XIII: 9.

Doctrinis variis et peregrinis nolite abduci. Optimum est enim gratia stabilire cor, non escis: quae non profuerunt ambulantibus in eis.

Be not led away with various and strange doctrines. For it is best that the heart be established with grace, not with meats; which have not profited those that walk in them.

1 Timothy VI: 20-21.

O Timothee, depositum custodi, devitans profanas vocum novitates, et oppositiones falsi nominis scientiae, Quam quidam promittentes, circa fidem exciderunt.

O Timothy, keep that which is committed to thy trust, avoiding the profane novelties of words, and oppositions of knowledge falsely so called. Which some promising, have erred concerning the faith.

Galatians I: 6-8.

Miror quod sic tam cito transferimini ab eo qui vos vocavit in gratiam Christi in aliud Evangelium: Quod non est aliud, nisi sunt aliqui qui vos conturbant, et volunt convertere Evangelium Christi. Sed licet nos aut angelus de caelo evangelizet vobis praeterquam quod evangelizavimus vobis, anathema sit.

I wonder that you are so soon removed from him that called you into the grace of Christ, unto another gospel. Which is not another, only there are some that trouble you, and would pervert the gospel of Christ. But though we, or an angel from heaven, preach a gospel to you besides that which we have preached to you, let him be anathema.

Jude I: 17-19; 16.

Vos autem carissimi, memores estote verborum, quae praedicta sunt ab apostolis Domini nostri Jesu Christi, Qui dicebant vobis, quoniam in novissimo tempore venient illusores, secundum desideria sua ambulantes in impietatibus. Hi sunt, qui segregant semetipsos, animales, Spiritum non habentes. Hi sunt murmuratores querulosi, secundum desideria sua ambulantes, et os eorum loquitur superba, mirantes personas quaestus causa.

But you, my dearly beloved, be mindful of the words which have been spoken before by the apostles of our Lord Jesus Christ, Who told you, that in the last time there should come mockers, walking according to their own desires in ungodlinesses. These are they, who separate themselves, sensual men, having not the Spirit. These are murmurers, full of complaints, walking according to their own desires, and their mouth speaketh proud things, admiring persons for gain's sake.

St. Augustine of Hippo, Doctor of the Church
De Fide ad Petrum; Ch. 38-40.

I. Firmissime tene et nullatenus dubites non solum omnes Paganos, sed etiam Judaeos, haereticos, atque schismaticos, qui extra Ecclesiam Catholicam praesentem finiunt vitam, in ignem aeternum ituros, qui paratus est diabolo et Angelis ejus.

I. You must firmly hold, and in nowise doubt, that not only the Pagans, but even Jews, heretics, and also schismatics, who end the present life outside the Catholic Church, are going to the eternal fire, which was prepared for the devil and his Angels.

II. Firmissime tene et nullatenus dubites quemlibet haereticum, sive schismaticum in nomine Patris et Filii, et Spiritus Sancti baptizatum, si Ecclesiae Catholicae non fuerit aggregatus, quantascumque eleëmosynas fecerit, etsi pro Christi nomine etiam sanguinem fuderit, nullatenus posse salvari. Omni enim homini, qui Ecclesiae Catholicae non tenet unitatem, neque baptismus, atque eleëmosyna quamlibet copiosa, neque mors pro nomine Christi suscepta proficere potest ad salutem, quamdiu in eo haeretica, vel schismatica pravitas perseverat, quae ducit ad mortem.

II. You must firmly hold, and in nowise doubt, that whichever heretic or schismatic who has been baptized in the name of the Father, and of the Son, and of the Holy Spirit, if he will not have been joined to the Catholic Church, whatsoever almsgiving he may have done, and even if he should shed his blood in the name of Christ, can in no manner be saved. Truly for every man, who does not keep the unity of the Catholic Church, neither baptism, nor almsgiving (no matter how abundant), nor death received in the name of Christ, can effect salvation, for as long as in the very matter, a heretical or schismatic

77

depravity should persevere, which leads to death.

III. Firmissime tene, et nullatenus dubites, non omnes qui intra Ecclesiam Catholicam baptizantur, accepturos esse vitam aeternam, sed eos qui percepto baptismate recte vivunt, id est, qui abstinuerunt se a vitiis et concupiscentiis carnis. Regnum enim coelorum sicut infideles, haeretici, atque schismatici non habebunt, sic Catholici criminosi possidere non poterunt.

III. You must firmly hold, and in nowise doubt, that not all who are baptized within the Catholic Church are going to be received into eternal life, rather those who live rightly after having received baptism, that is, who have kept themselves away from vices and the concupiscence of the flesh. Indeed, as infidels, heretics and schismatics will not have the kingdom of heaven, likewise criminal Catholics cannot possess it.

Sit nomen Domini Benedictum in saecula. Amen.

Made in the USA
Columbia, SC
22 December 2020

29687664R00048